T0196548

Evie's

DELECTABLE
EDIBLES

Eve Theresa Marie Carter

authorHOUSE®

AuthorHouse™
1663 Liberty Drive
Bloomington, IN 47403
www.authorhouse.com
Phone: 1 (800) 839-8640

Published by AuthorHouse   05/09/2016

ISBN: 978-1-5246-0192-8 (sc)
ISBN: 978-1-5246-0191-1 (e)

This book is dedicated to
My beautiful daughter:
Lynn Alexandra Nygaard

APPETIZERS AND DIPS

Spinach Dip

1 package fresh spinach, washed, cooked and drained well or
1 package frozen spinach, chopped and well drained
1 cup sour-cream
1 cup mayonnaise
1- 5 ounce can of water chestnuts, chopped
3 to 4 green onions chopped
1 package of dry leek soup mix

Cook spinach, squeeze dry and chop finely. Chop all remaining ingredients.

Refrigerate until serving time, preferably overnight to blend flavours.

Just before serving, take a slice off the top of a loaf of unsliced pumpernickel bread.

Scoop out center and break bread into bite sized chunks for dipping.
Fill hollowed out loaf with dip.

Have an extra loaf ready to break up more chunks, as well as one or two knives for spreading the dip onto the chunks, or cutting up then serve on a serving dish.

With a little bit of sugar and a little bit of love, will make anyone's day brighter.

Bruschetta In A Bowl

Cubed day old Italian Bread 4 cups (1 Litre)
1/3 cup Balsamic vinegar
Medium cucumber with peel, quartered lengthwise and sliced
I medium red or yellow pepper, chopped
1 medium roma tomato
3 diced freshly ground pepper
¼ finely chopped fresh sweet basil
¼ cup sliced pitted ripe olives
2 teaspoons olive oil

Spread bread cubes on large ungreased baking sheet with sides. Bake in 350 Degree oven for 5 minutes. Stir. Bake for 10 to 15 minutes. Until toasted. Combine remaining 8 ingredients in large bowl. Add bread cubes. Toss. Makes 7 cups (1.7 L) enough for 7 servings.

EASY ANTIPASTO

2 cans flaked tuna
1 jar chopped green olives
1 can chopped mushrooms
1 small jar sweet mixed pickles, chopped fine
1 – 16 ounce bottle ketchup
1 – 12 ounce bottle of chili sauce

Mix all ingredients and refrigerate. Serve with crackers.

When you think all is lost, just remember to call : Candy Man Can.

HOT SEAFOOD DIP

1 – 8 ounce package cream cheese
6 -Tablespoons mayonnaise
1 minced onion
1/2 teaspoon prepared mustard
2 - Tablespoons chili sauce
1 -Tablespoon chopped fresh parsley or 1 teaspoon flakes
1 - 6 ounce can crab, lobster or shrimp

Melt over medium heat and fold in 1 – 6 ounce can seafood.
Top with fine buttered bread crumbs.
Bake 25 minutes at 375 degree F.
Serve with crackers.

Don't get into too many spirits, they may come back to haunt you.

HAM AND CHEESE BALL

8 ounce's cream cheese
1/4 cup mayonnaise
measure enough ham to equal 2 cups
2 Tablespoons parsley flakes
1 teaspoon minced onion
1/4 teaspoon dry mustard
1/4 teaspoon Tabasco sauce
(Optional) 1/2 cup chopped nuts

Beat cheese and mayonnaise until smooth.

Stir in all the rest of the ingredients, except for the nuts.

Cover and chill for a few hours, form into 2 balls, roll in the nuts.

Freezes well. Excellent on any type of cracker.

VEGGIE DIP

1 cup plain yogurt
1/3 cup mayonnaise
1 Tablespoon chopped onion
1 teaspoon dill weed
1 Tablespoon chopped parsley
1 teaspoon seasoning salt
1 teaspoon dry mustard

Combine all ingredients in a bowl and mix well. Place in a plastic container.

Serve with carrot sticks, celery sticks, cherry tomatoes, radishes, zucchini and so on.

Makes almost 1 and 1/4 cups.

A true man is kind of hard to find, yet if you look hard-enough. He may be right in front of you.

EASY CHEESE BALL

250 grams cream cheese
250 grams cold pack cheddar cheese
1/2 cup butter
100 gram slivered almonds for top

Mix all ingredients together. Shape into a roll or log.

Toast and sprinkle top with almonds or whatever kind of nuts you prefer.

CRAB CHEESE BALL

1 can of fresh crab meat
2 large pkg. Cream cheese
7 or 8 drops Worcestershire sauce
1 – 1/2 Tablespoon lemon juice

TOPPING

2 Tablespoons horseradish
1/4 cup ketchup
1 to 2 drops of Tabasco sauce
5 to 6 drops Worcestershire sauce

Beat cream and mayonnaise together until smooth.

Then add remaining 4 ingredients.

Then add rest of ingredients, taste and shape into ball.

Mix topping ingredients (taste) together.

Please don't sneeze onto my crab-balls. They may roll right into your lap.

SAVORY POTATO SKINS

4 - large baking potatoes, baked
3 - Tablespoons melted butter
1 to 2 teaspoons salt
1 teaspoon garlic powder
1 teaspoon paprika
Sour-cream and chives

Cut and bake potatoes in half lengthwise. Scoop out pulp, leaving 1/4 inch thick shells.

Cut shells into quarters and place on greased cookie sheets.

Brush inside with butter. Combine salt, garlic powder and paprika.

Sprinkle over skins. Broil until golden brown, 5 to 7 minutes.

Serve with sour cream and chives.

Never let a thick skinned person get the better of you! Your skin might be brighter than theirs.

CRAB STUFFED MUSHROOMS

40 bite sized or 20 to 25 large mushrooms | 1/4 cup shredded cheddar cheese

1 – Tablespoon butter or margarine | 4 – 3/4 oz, crab or crab leg, cut up, membrane vein removed

2 –teaspoons all-purpose flour

1 garlic clove, shredded | 1 to 2 teaspoon onion

A pinch of paprika

1/4 cup rich milk or cream | 1/2 to 1 cup shredded Monterey Jack cheese

1 Tablespoon lemon juice

1 Tablespoon salad dressing

Remove mushroom stems. Melt butter in saucepan. Stir in flour. Add garlic, milk, lemon juice and salad dressing, stirring until mixture boils and thickens.

Add cheddar cheese, stir to melt. Stir in crab and onion. Fill mushroom caps. Sprinkle Monterey Jack cheese over top.

BAKE at 400 degree F (200 C) for 15 minutes or until heated through.

When crossing the road make sure you take giant steps, for if you don't you may not get to the other side.

SHRIMP DIP

4 ounces pkg, softened cream cheese 1/2 tsp. Worcestershire sauce

1 cup dairy sour cream 1 Tbsp. Ketchup

1 tsp. Onion salt 1 tsp. Lemon juice

1 tsp. Prepared horseradish

Beat cheese until smooth, then gradually beat in sour cream.

Mix in onion salt, horseradish, Worcestershire sauce, ketchup and lemon juice.

Rinse shrimp and devein if necessary, flake. Blend into sour cream mixture. Chill 2 hours. Makes about 2 cups.

MY FAVORITE GOLDEN DIP FOR VEGETABLES

1 cup mayonnaise 5 ml Worcestershire sauce

25 ml curry powder 2 ml celery salt

5 ml lemon juice Dash of cayenne

Mix all ingredients together.

VEGETABLE DIP

2/3 cup mayonnaise 2/3 cup sour-cream

1 Tablespoon celery seed 1 Tablespoon parsley

1 Tablespoon dill 1 Tablespoon minced onion

Dash lemon pepper to taste

Mix all ingredients together. Let stand 2 hours before serving

When all else fails make sure you find your balance again.

MY FAVORITE FRUIT DIP

1 cup crushed pineapple

3/4 cup angel flake coconut

1 small vanilla yogurt

1 pkg. Dream whip

1 small pkg. Vanilla pudding

3/4 cup milk

Mix pudding and coconut together.
Add remaining ingredients together and blend. Refrigerate overnight.

LIGHT AND FABULOUS

2 cups of any flavor yogurt

whip cream to match 2 cups of yogurt

1 package of gelatin

pink food color

1 cup of any type of fresh fruit

Mix all together, this can be used as a fruit dip, or eaten as a light calorie dessert. Great for people with diabetic issues.

May good thoughts enter into your mind, then others will like you even more.

SHRIMP COCKTAIL SAUCE

2/3 cup ketchup
3 tablespoons chili sauce (or to taste)
2 tablespoons horseradish
3 tablespoons lemon juice (or to taste)
Dash cayenne
Dash Tabasco

Blend all together and refrigerate.

Whenever you need a little help just call Candy Man 911.

CAESAR SALAD DRESSING

Yields I cup olive oil solidifies when stored in the fridge. If the dressing becomes solid, hold under warm water for a minute or two. Cool before serving.

1 egg yolk 1/4 cup lemon juice or use lime juice if preferred 60ml
2 to 3 anchovy fillets 2 to 3 garlic cloves chopped
1/2 teaspoon salt or substitute 2ml
1/4 black pepper 1 ml
2/3 cup extra-virgin olive oil 150 ml

Place egg yolk in food processor along with lemon juice, anchovies, garlic, salt, pepper and blend for at least 1 minute or until pureed.

Slowly, add oil in steady stream into processor while still on high speed. Scrape sides of bowl and blend for another 30 seconds.

Transfer dressing into jar and refrigerator for up to one week.

If you ever make a slip; don't get caught up with your lip.

SALAD DRESSING FOR POTATO SALAD

2 cups Miracle Whip or I cup Miracle whip and mix with I cup Mayonnaise
2 and 1/2 teaspoons mustard
Salt optional, I prefer to use seasoning salt to taste.
1 teaspoon Parsley flakes

Mix all together and put in jar and keep in refrigerator, will keep for weeks.

SALAD DRESSING FOR MACARONI SALAD

2 cups Miracle Whip or 1 cup of Miracle Whip and mix with 1 cup Mayonnaise
1/2 teaspoon dill pickle juice 1 teaspoon lemon juice
Seasoning Salt to taste Parsley flakes or Dill for added taste
Sugar optional
Mix all together and put in jar and keep in refrigerator, will keep for weeks.

When entering into a bus make sure you bring a nose clip, you don't want to know how everyone smells.

OIL AND LEMON DRESSING

Yield 1 cup

Flaxseed oil contains 57% Omega 3 essential fatty acids by weight. This precious and essential dietary oil is absolutely vital to health. A Canadian recommendation for flax-seed oil is 1 teaspoon per day.

2/3 cup flaxseed oil or extra-virgin olive oil or mixture of broth	150 ml
5 tbsp. Freshly squeezed lemon juice	75 ml
1/4 tsp. Salt	1 ml
pinch pepper	

Mix all ingredients in a jar and shake vigorously for 1 minute.

If possible, let sit for one hour or longer to allow the flavours to blend together.

When you think all is lost, try putting on a few pounds of laughter.

COLESLAW DRESSING

1 cup mayonnaise   3/4 cup sugar

1/4 cup oil or olive oil   1/4 teaspoon of salt and pepper

4 cups or more of shredded cabbage. You can add 1/4 cup diced apple or shredded carrots.

Add all to shredded coleslaw mixture.

CREAMY CHIVE DRESSING

Yields 2 cups
This dressing is very suitable during the hot summer months.
The cucumber is very cooling and provides clean taste to the palate.

1- 10 oz. package softened tofu 300 grams
1 cup cucumber, chopped 250 ml
2 tbsp. Flaxseed oil 30 ml
2 tbsp. Chives or green onion 30 ml
1/2 tsp. Salt 2 ml
pinch pepper

Empty contents of tofu package into blender.

Add cucumber and flaxseed oil and blend for 15 seconds. Add chives, salt, pepper and blend for 5 seconds. Keeps in refrigerator for up to one week.

Don't ever think that a mighty mouse can eat off the same plate as you!

DRESSING

5 cups vinegar

4 cups white sugar

1 teaspoon mustard seed

1 tablespoon turmeric

3 cups water

1 teaspoon celery seed

6 tablespoons dry mustard

1 cup flour

Mix flour, mustard and turmeric with a little vinegar. Heat rest of vinegar with sugar, mustard and celery seed. Add mixture and pickles. Cook 20 minutes and seal in sterilized jars.

Please remember never add a little lip to all your ingredients.

ANNE'S BASIC SALSA

Yields 3 cups
A salsa need not only be served with corn chips. Try this basic salsa recipe and the following variations on top of baked bean and corn loaf.

1 – ½ cups tomatoes, diced	375 ml
3/4 cup red onions, diced	180 ml
3/4 cup red, green and or yellow bell peppers, diced	180 ml
1 jalapeno pepper seeds removed, minced	1
1/4 cup parsley and or cilantro, chopped	60 ml
1 1/2 tbs. Lemon juice	30 ml
2 tbsp. Olive oil	30 ml
1 1/2 tsp. Ground cumin	7 ml
salt and pepper to taste	

In medium mixing bowl, mix all ingredients together.

Adjust the seasonings.

Refrigerate for at least 3 hours before serving.

When a grain of salt has been dropped in front of you, don't lick it up.

FRESH CUCUMBER YOGURT SAUCE

½ cup grated English cucumber with peel
¼ teaspoon salt
Low-fat plain yogurt
Garlic cloves, minced
Chopped fresh mint leaves or parsley

Combine cucumber and salt in small bowl. Let stand for 10 minutes. Pour into sieve.

Squeeze cucumber until most of liquid is gone. Return to bowl. Add remaining 3 ingredients.

Stir gently, cover. Chill for up to 1 hour or more for flavors to blend. Makes 1 ½ cups.

ITALIAN COATING MIX

Add 2 tablespoons grated Parmesan cheese
1/2 teaspoon oregano
Add this to one recipe plain coating mix. (make your own coating mix of flour, spices and a little of finely crushed crackers)
Moisten chicken pieces with water
Shake one piece at a time until evenly coated.

Bake in 400 -degree F oven for 30-40 minutes.

Never take a break away from your husband, he might break an egg.

COATING MIXES

For oven-fried chicken, etc

Combine 1/2 cup baking powder biscuit mix
1 tablespoon dried parsley
1/2 teaspoon salt
1 teaspoon paprika
1/2 teaspoon onion salt
1/2 teaspoon thyme
1/2 teaspoon garlic salt

Store at room temperature in air-tight container or plastic bag.

Telling the absolute truth, may bring a softness into your beautiful heart.

MARINADE FOR MEAT

Use oil and lemon dressing
Add 1/2 cup tomato juice or V8
1/2 teaspoon Italian seasoning or make your own
Tobasco Sause (optional) to taste
Pinch of pepper (white pepper)

Refrigerate overnight, use to merinade with beef

Note: This is excellent with wild meat

When you see a wild man, do not attempt to bicker; he might sneeze on you.

SALADS

BROCCOLI SALAD

1 cup salad dressing

1 tablespoon vinegar

6 slices bacon, crisply fried and crumbled

1/4 cup chopped green onion

I prefer using red onion

1 cup grated cheddar cheese

1/4 cup sugar

1 large bunch broccoli cut up

Method:

Mix salad dressing, sugar and vinegar together, set aside. In a separate bowl mix broccoli, bacon, green or red onion and 3/4 cup cheese. Pour dressing mixture over top and mix. Sprinkle with remaining cheese.

Never stare and wrinkle your nose at a man taking your picture.

BROCCOLI SALAD DELIGHT

1 bunch of broccoli, chopped   1/2 cup chopped celery

1/2 cup chopped red onions

1 cup mayonnaise   1 tablespoon wine vinegar

1/8 cup sugar   6 slices bacon crisply fried and crumbled

Method:

Combine vegetables in a large bowl. In a separate bowl combine mayonnaise, vinegar, sugar and mix well. Pour over vegetables and chill well. May be garnished with bacon bits before serving.

Always stay on the good side of things, negativity will get you no where.

TACO SALAD

1 to 2 pounds of hamburger	1 envelope seasoned taco mix
1 small lettuce shredded	3 tomatoes diced
1 onion chopped	1 can kidney beans drained
2 cups grated cheddar cheese	
Corn, tortilla or taco chips	1 cucumber chopped
2 to 3 stalks celery chopped	1 green onion diced or red onion
1 green pepper diced	Fresh mushrooms

Cook hamburger in frying pan until crumbly and no longer pink.

Season with taco mix. Drain well and cool. In a large bowl mix the hamburger with remaining ingredients. Toss well. A dressing made with oil, lemon juice and salt can be poured on and tossed; or use a dressing of your choice just before serving. This mixture can be put into Taco shells.

In any given situation, never swear at your spouse, he might bite harder than you.

FRESH MUSHROOM SALAD

4 cups of fresh mushrooms, sliced or leave whole
1/4 cup or less of vinegar (to taste) 2 Tablespoons of Olive Oil
1/4 cup soya sauce (to taste) fresh garlic chopped or
1 teaspoon garlic salt
Fresh parsley

Coat mushrooms evenly and let sit for two or three hours before serving.

Serve on a bed of fresh lettuce.

DILLED MUSHROOM SALAD

3 to 4 cups of fresh mushrooms   1 clove of garlic, diced
1 cup of diced celery   1/4 cup of diced red onion
1 small cucumber or even use 1 dill pickle
1 to 2 tablespoons of dill pickle juice or use fresh dill added with
vinegar, fresh thyme, olive oil, cayenne to taste, white pepper.

Variation: Use my Italian dressing, oh so yummy.

Never stand in front of a moving vehicle, it may be fully loaded.

MACARONI SALAD

Cook 2 to 3 cups elbow macaroni
1 cup cooked ham
¾ cup cheddar cheese cubed
½ cup cooked frozen peas
½ cup chopped onion
½ cup chopped celery

Dressing:
½ cup Kraft miracle whip
½ cup mayonnaise
1 tablespoon mustard
Add about 1 teaspoon dill pickle juice for added flavor
Sprinkle some seasoning salt over top then add this to the ingredients for the salad.

Never get into a food fight with a mad bull, he may charge right at you with evil intent.

YOGURT DRESSED BEET SALAD

2 to 3 large beets, roasted and cut up into eighths
Yogurt Dressing:
1/2 cup Fat Greek Yogurt
2 Tablespoons cider vinegar
1 Tablespoon Gold Honey
1 Tablespoon Lemon juice
1 tablespoon Dijon mustard
2 tablespoon chopped tarragon
cider vinegar salt

Vinegar Mixture:
4 Tablespoon white wine vinegar
1/3 cup Organic Olive Oil
1/3 cup Pure cold compressed Canola Oil
Salt
1 tablespoon Black Peppercorns, coarsely crushed
1 lemon, zest and juice
1 head romaine heart, trimmed of outer leaves and julienned
Salt

In medium bowl, combine yogurt, cider vinegar, honey, lemon juice, Dijon mustard and chopped tarragon. Whisk ingredients together until evenly combined. Adjust seasonings with touch of cider vinegar and a pinch of salt if required. Set aside.

In small mixing bowl, whisk together the white vinegar, olive oil and canola oil. Add a pinch of salt to taste.

To assemble spoon a few large spoonfuls of yogurt dressing onto a serving plate. In a separate bowl, toss beets with enough of the vinegar mixture to season and dress evenly. Drop beets on top of the yogurt and sprinkle with crushed black peppercorns and lemon zest.

In another bowl, dress the julienned romaine with the lemon juice and sprinkle of salt. Toss lettuce to coat evenly. Then top beets with the romaine. Serves two as a starter salad.

Always remember when using vinegar as a dressing, don't inhale it as if it were tossed with gas.

WALDORF SPINACH

Toasted pecan pieces
¾ cup medium red apple with peel, cored and sliced into thin wedges
Medium orange, peeled (white pith removed) halved and thinly sliced
Red onion, thinly sliced and separated
½ cup bag of fresh spinach
2 – 10 ounce 285 g each torn into bite size

Dressing
¼ cup Granulated sugar
½ teaspoon dry mustard
1/8 teaspoon hot pepper sauce
¼ cup white vinegar
¼ cup cooking oil

Reserve ¼ cup (60 ml) pecans, apple, orange, red onion and spinach in large bowl.

Dressing:
Combine reserved pecans, sugar, mustard, hot pepper sauce, vinegar and cooking oil in blender. Process for 2 minutes until smooth. Pour over spinach mixture. Toss to coat salad.

Never coat or quote all ingredients with anxiety or a mean streak of anger with intolerable cruelty. Spinach might come back and bite you.

MEAT FISH AND POULTRY DISHES

BEEF

My Father's Favourite Bullets

Meaning (Meatballs)

1 cup finely chopped onion
An equal measure of salt and pepper
2 to 3 pounds of hamburger
Enough flour to mix into hamburger
1 to 2 eggs
braze meatballs with olive oil or canola oil

This is the way the old natives used to cook without any real seasonings.

Cook or bake for at least twenty minutes, turn down heat and cook slow on low heat.

The oil gives these meatballs a flavour all of its own especially if you cook over an open outdoor fire.

If cooking out doors make sure you don't go running into the house and watch TV.

KEFTETHES

1-1/2 pounds minced meat
4 ounces soft bread crumbs (moisten in milk)
3 small minced onions
2 well -beaten eggs
Parsley
1- Teaspoon chopped mint
1-Tablespoon grated cheese
Salt and Pepper
Flour
Olive oil or butter for frying pan.
Enough lemon to moisten.
Combine let stand for 30 minutes. Dust with flour. Fry

With a little added sugar you may not look so sour.

MEAT PIE

Can be frozen

Heat 2 Tablespoons lard or other shortening.
Add 1 pound minced lean beef and 1 cup chopped onions
Cook and stir until brown and add 1 cup shredded raw carrot.
1 teaspoon salt
1/4 teaspoon pepper
1/2 teaspoon sugar
Stir in 1/4 cup ketchup
1 cup water
2 teaspoons prepared mustard
Cover and simmer slowly, stir often for 15 minutes.
Cool
Bake in two crusts in 425 degree (Hot) oven for 40 minutes.

When you look down a ladder, make sure your man doesn't land on you.

SWEET AND SOUR MEATBALLS

Sauce: Combine in a saucepan
1 tablespoon lemon juice
2 tablespoons sugar (brown sugar) optional
3/4 cup water
1-1/2 tomato juice
Cover and bring to a boil.

Meatballs:
1 -pound lean beef
2 tablespoons onion grated
1 egg
Salt and pepper

Mix well and shape into meatballs. Put sauce in a 2- quart casserole and drop meatballs.

Cover and bake in 325 -degree oven for at least 1 hour. Serves 4.

Make sure you don't clap too loud, for a woodpecker will start pecking at your window.

BEEF DIANE

8-12 slices rare roast beef
3- tablespoons butter
8- mushrooms sliced
1-tablespoon lemon juice
3-tablespoons gravy or 1 beef bouillon cube dissolved in
1/4 -cup boiling water
1-tablespoon Worcestershire sauce
3-tablespoons red wine or brandy
Salt and Pepper to taste

Heat beef slices slowly in butter. Place on heated platter. Brown mushrooms in remaining butter. Add rest of ingredients and heat until bubbling. Pour hot sauce over slices.
Serves 4-6

When entering into a polar-bear shop don't breathe on him, he may break wind.

SHIPWRECK

1 to 1/12 lb hamburger 1 cup tomato soup
1 good sized onion, sliced 1 soup can water
3 to 4 potatoes, sliced 1 can corn
1/2 cup rice, precooked Salt, garlic, and pepper to taste
Optional: 2 diced carrots

Put layers of sliced potatoes, onion, carrots and corn in buttered baking dish.

Season with all seasonings. Mix uncooked hamburger with cooked rice, salt and pepper. Spread this mixture over the vegetables. Combine the tomato soup and water and pour over hamburger mixture. Cover and bake at 350 F for 2 hours.

When walking along a long endless road, make sure you never skip over a live-wire.

STROGANOFF MEAT BALLS

2 pounds ground beef 1 cup bread crumbs
1 cup water 2 teaspoons salt
1/2 teaspoon pepper

In large bowl mix beef, crumbs, water, salt and pepper.
Shape into about 40 meat balls. Put on cookie sheet with sides.
Bake at 425 Degree oven for 15 minutes. Put all in deep casserole.

2 cups water 1 finely chopped onion
1/4 cup beef soup base 1 teaspoon salt 1/4 teaspoon pepper

In medium saucepan put water, onion, soup powder, salt and pepper.
Bring to a boil.

4 tablespoons cornstarch 1/4 cup water 1 – 10 oz. can sliced mushrooms

1- 10 oz. can cream of mushroom soup 2 teaspoons parsley flakes

1/4 teaspoon paprika 2 cups sour-cream

In a small bowl stir cornstarch in water, pour into boiling liquid stirring until thickened.

Stir in mushrooms soup, parsley, paprika and sour cream. If to thick stir in a bit of water.

Pour over meatballs. Cover. Bake at 350 Degree oven for 25 to 30 minutes.
Serves 6

Hello mister, have you seen my dog walking this way? Well no young lad he was walking this way!

Mindless Meat Sauce

1 ½ pounds lean ground beef
¼ teaspoon sage
¼ teaspoon oregano
1 tablespoon salt
½ teaspoon pepper
1 medium onion, finely chopped
15 large mushrooms, finely chopped
3 cloves garlic minced
1 28 -ounce can tomatoes chopped with juice
1 10 -ounce can tomato sauce
1-5 ½ ounce can tomato paste

Preheat oven to 350 Degree. In large roasting pan, spread ground beef.

Cook for 30 minutes, stirring occasionally to separate. Meanwhile combine sage, oregano, salt, pepper, onion, mushrooms and garlic in saucepan and cook at medium heat until onions are transparent. Spread over meat and continue cooking in oven for 15 minutes. Remove from oven and add canned tomatoes, tomato sauce, paste and V8 juice. Bring to boil then simmer for 1 hour or longer. Add salt to taste. Store in container and freeze.

Never stare a bull in the eye, he may make contact with you.

CHICKEN

BARBEQUE CHICKEN WINGS

1 - pound chicken wings

Sauce:

1 cup water	½ cup brown sugar
¼ cup vinegar	½ cup ketchup
Paprika	Tabasco sauce
Salt	

Roll chicken wings in flour and pan brown. Bring sauce ingredients to a boil. Pour over wings and bake in oven until done, about 1 hour.

HONEY BAKED CHICKEN

1 chicken 2 – 2 1/2 pounds	
1/2 teaspoon salt	3 tablespoons butter
1/4 cup prepared mustard	1/3 cup honey
1 Tablespoon fresh lime juice	1 teaspoon salt

Preheat oven to 350 Degree. Melt butter in shallow baking dish pan. Sprinkle with 1/2 teaspoon salt. Combine honey and other ingredients. Bake 30 minutes, brushing with honey mixture. Turn, bake 20- 25 minutes longer and keep brushing.

Never go to sleep with an angry attitude, this will make more age lines more prominent.

CHICKEN CACCIATORE

(Serves 4)

4 -pounds chicken cut up	2 – 3 tablespoons flour
1/4 olive oil	2 pounds chopped shallots
1 minced garlic clove	1/2 cup dry white wine
1 teaspoon salt	1/4 cup tomato paste
1/4 teaspoon pepper	12 bay leaf
3/4 cup chicken stock	1/8 teaspoon thyme
1/2 – 1 cup sliced mushrooms	1/8 teaspoon sweet marjoram
2 tablespoons brandy or your choice	

Dredge chicken in the flour. Brown with shallots, garlic in oil.

Add remaining ingredients. Simmer covered, for 1 hour until chicken is tender.

Serve over spaghetti.

Try hopping on one foot, this may take away your hiccups. If it doesn't breathe into a brown paper bag.

CHICKEN CASSEROLE

I chicken (fryer) cut up   1 pkg. Cream mushroom soup

1 cup long grain rice   1 pkg. Onion soup

1 – 1/2 cups rich milk

Place chicken in a greased casserole dish. Mix all ingredients and pour over chicken.

Bake 1 hour uncovered and one more hour covered with tin foil.

CHICKEN POT BARLEY

Fry or saute cut up chicken breast 3 to 4 chunks

1 onion diced   1 green pepper   4 stalks of celery

2 large carrots   ¼ cup of fresh or frozen peas

Seasoning Salt to taste   ¼ teaspoon pepper

Add fresh parsley or dried parsley flakes

What enhances the flavor is vegetable seasoning

¼ cup of barley

(Optional) 2 large or medium sized potatoes

(Optional) as yet a sweet potato gives it another type of flavoring.

Add all in a rectangular baking sauce pan

This can be baked as a casserole or even used as a heavy soup. Bake for ¾ to 1 hour in oven.

Serve with hot biscuits or bread.

When you wake up every morning make sure you smile at yourself in the mirror; then everything will look like a bed or roses.

CURRY CHICKEN

6- Skinned and boned chicken breasts
(Boil until tender)
1 cup mayonnaise
1 teaspoon curry (to taste)
1- 8 ounce package noodles or pasta
1 -can cream of mushroom soup
1 tablespoon lemon juice
1 ½ cup shredded cheddar cheese

Combine all ingredients (except ½ cup shredded cheese) and pour into buttered Baking dish. Chicken breasts on top of noodle mixture. Sprinkle with rest of cheese And bake at 350 degree oven for 30 minutes.

Serve with broccoli or another vegetable. Also serve with warm bread rolls.

Remember never lie down with too many sleeping dogs, they may all howl endlessly through the night.

EVIE'S CURRIED CHICKEN

4 to 5 chicken breasts skinned and deveined
Cut into slivered pieces
Dip breasts into ¼ to ½ cup of milk

1 teaspoon or suit to your taste curry powder
1 tablespoon seasoning salt
¼ teaspoon pepper
½ teaspoon parsley flakes
½ teaspoon onion powder or dry onion flakes
Pinch of paprika
1 to 1 ½ cups flour or double seasonings and flour to make bigger batch

Coat chicken breasts with seasoning mix. Bake in oven till golden brown.

Serve all with fresh crisp broccoli. Also to add an extra kind of taste, fry or
Bake some bacon and add to the chicken roasting in oven.

When dancing in the park, make sure you wear sandals or shoes. You may
need them for some support.

HONEY CHICKEN AND NUT STIR FRY

1 - pound boneless chicken breasts

¾ cup orange juice

1/3 cup honey

3 tablespoons soya sauce

1 tablespoon cornstarch

¼ - teaspoon ground ginger

2 tablespoon vegetable oil (divided)

2 large carrots, diagonally cut

2 stalks celery, diagonally cut

½ cup cashews or peanuts

Hot rice

Cut chicken into thin strips and set aside. In a small bowl, combine orange juice, Honey, soya sauce, cornstarch, and ginger. Mix well. Heat I tablespoon of oil in a Large skillet over medium heat. Add carrots and celery. Stir-fry about 3 minutes. Remove vegetables and set aside. Pour remaining oil into skillet. Add sauce mixture and nuts. Cook and stir over medium heat until sauce is thickened. Serve over hot rice. Makes about 4 to 6 servings.

SAVORY PASTRY FOR CHICKEN POT PIE

Pastry

2 cups sifted flour

½ teaspoon paprika

Pinch of nutmeg

1 teaspoon salt

½ teaspoon celery seeds

2/3 cup lard

¼ cup ice cold water

Filling

1 cup frozen mixed vegetables or cut up your own vegetables

¼ cup margarine

1 medium onion, chopped

½ pound fresh mushrooms, sliced

1/3 cup flour

½ cup water

1 chicken bouillon cube

3 cups cooked diced chicken

1 cup cream style cottage cheese

1/3 cup parsley

1 teaspoon salt

¼ teaspoon pepper

½ teaspoon marjoram

¼ teaspoon poultry seasoning

Mix flour and seasonings together with a fork. Add lard and cut into coarsely with pastry blender. Sprinkle in water, I tablespoon at a time. Try not to add any extra Water. Gather into a ball and press firmly. Divide into 2 parts. Flatten slightly with Hands and roll into pie shape; place in pie pan.

Filling

Bring vegetables to boil. Drain immediately. Saute onions and mushrooms in margarine for approximately 3 minutes. Sprinkle in flour and stir to blend. Remove from heat. Stir in water, return to medium heat. Stir in vegetables and remaining ingredients.

Fill with meat filling. Cover with remaining pastry and seal edge. Make slits in top. Bake 35 to 40 minutes at 425 Degree oven.

Never bite off more than you can handle.

PORK

SWEET AND SOUR SPARE RIBS

3 – 1/2 pounds spareribs in 2 inch squares
2 large onions sliced
1/3 cup brown sugar
1/2 cup vinegar
1 tablespoon soya sauce
2/3 cup canned pineapple juice
1/3 cup water
1/2 teaspoon salt
1/8 teaspoon pepper
1 tablespoon cornstarch
1 tablespoon water
cooked hot fluffy rice
Vary: 1 cup drained can pineapple chunks

Preheat boil 10 minutes. Place spareribs in boiler pan, sprinkle with salt and pepper.

Broil till brown on both sides. Place onions in Dutch oven or kettle, with 2 teaspoons pork fat from broiler, saute 2 minutes, add brown sugar, vinegar, soya sauce, pineapple juice, 1/3 cup water, salt, pepper and ribs. Cover simmer over low heat for 2 hours. Remove ribs, thicken sauce in saucepan with cornstarch dissolved in 1 tablespoon cold water, replace ribs in sauce. Serve over rice.

Serves 6

May you never meet up with a gambler, you might have to give him your shirt.

DRY RIBS

7 1/2 pounds cubed meat or use cut up ribs

1 3/4 cups white sugar

1/4 cup brown sugar	1 ounce MSG
1/2 cup Lawry's seasoning salt	1 3/4 teaspoon salt

Sprinkle with garlic salt or powder. Marinate 8 hours or overnight. Roll in flour and deep fry or bake on low temperature.

ITALIAN PORK CHOPS

6 pork chops	3 tablespoons fat
2 – 1/2 cups tomatoes	1/2 cup water
1/4 cup rice	1 cup chopped onions
1 small green pepper chopped	1 teaspoon prepared mustard
1 teaspoon sugar	1/2 teaspoon salt
1/8 teaspoon pepper	

Brown the chops in the hot fat, transfer to a deep saucepan, add remaining ingredients. Cover and simmer 1 – 1/4 hours or until tender. Serve with the tomato rice mixture as sauce.

When you think all is lost try looking in your back pocket.

BRAISED PORK CHOPS

4 to 6 trimmed pork chops left over bacon drippings
Season pork chops with cayenne pepper
Mild mustard portion to taste
To make the crackers cling to chops coat crackers with ¼ cup milk and one egg
Add to the pork chops
Salt and pepper to taste
Coat pork chops with finely chopped dried crackers

To enhance flavor add a touch of lemon juice or accent

Fry in bacon drippings till golden brown. Then put in oven and bake till done
Garnish with any type of greens to which you prefer.

Heat oven to 325 Degree, before you put pork chops in.
Enjoy

Make every day the best day of your life, for things will look beautiful within a happy eyes and face.

PINEAPPLE PORK

¾ pounds Lean boneless pork loin, trimmed and thinly sliced
1 teaspoons canola oil
½ teaspoon ground ginger
½ teaspoon paprika
Freshly ground pepper sprinkle

1 medium carrots, thinly sliced on diagonal
½ medium green pepper, cut into large slivers
½ red pepper, cut into large slivers
1 small onion, sliced lengthwise into wedges

14 ounces -can of pineapple tidbits, juice reserved
2 – white vinegar
1 tablespoon brown sugar, packed

¼ cup reserved pineapple juice
1 tablespoon low-sodium soya sauce
1 tablespoon ketchup
2 – 1/8 tablespoon cornstarch

Saute pork in canola in large frying pan for 1 minute. Sprinkle with paprika, ginger and pepper. Saute until no pink remains in pork.
Stir in next 4 ingredients.

Reserve ¼ cup pineapple juice. Set aside. Add remaining juice and pineapple to pork mixture. Drizzle with vinegar. Sprinkle with brown sugar. Stir. Bring to a boil.

Cover and simmer for 30 minutes until carrots are tender.

Combine reserved juice, soya sauce, ketchup and cornstarch in small bowl until smooth. Stir in pork mixture. Heat and stir until boiling and thickened. Makes about 5 ¼ cups. Serves 4 people.

Never keep a frown on your face all day, someone might try to frown back at you with full force.

STUFFED FRUIT PORK LION

2 ¼ pounds lean boneless pork tenderloin, trimmed
(about 8x4x2 inch, 20x10x5 cm, size)
14 ounces can of unsweetened applesauce
1 Garlic cloves, minced
¼ teaspoon salt
2 tablespoons brown sugar, packed
1/8 teaspoon ground cinnamon
1/16 teaspoon ground nutmeg
2 cups boiling water
1 cup dried fruit (such as apricots, prunes and cranberries), diced

2 teaspoons Canola oil
1 tablespoon Dried mixed herbs
1 garlic clove, minced (Optional)
Generous sprinkle of ground pepper
¼ cup white wine (or apple juice), optional

SAUCE

2 tablespoons cornstarch
¼ cup sherry (or non-alcohol sherry)
½ teaspoon ground cinnamon

Butterfly tenderloin by cutting horizontally lengthwise, not quite through center.
Open flat. Pound with mallet or rolling pin to an even thickness.

Combine 1/3 cup applesauce with garlic and salt in small bowl. Spread on cut side of pork. Set aside remaining applesauce.

Combine sugar, cinnamon, nutmeg and boiling water in medium bowl. Add dried fruit. Soak for 10 minutes. Drain, reserving liquid. Pack fruit onto pork in even layer, leaving about 1 inch (2.5 cm) from edges on all 4 sides uncovered. Roll jelly roll fashion. Tie with butcher's string or use metal skewers to secure.

Combine canola oil, herbs, garlic, pepper and 1 tablespoon (reserved applesauce in small dish. Coat pork. Place on rack in small roaster or pan with sides. Add white wine to bottom of roaster. Cover in 325 Degree (160C) oven for about 1 ¼ hours until internal temperature reaches 160 Degree (75). Remove from oven

SAUCE:

Combine cornstarch and reserved liquid in small saucepan. Add remaining applesauce (about 1 ¼ cups, 300 ml) and sherry. Heat and stir on medium until boiling and thickened. Makes about 2 ½ cups (650 ml) sauce.

At the end of the day never go to sleep while your still mad at your partner.

CURRIED HAM

1 tablespoon butter or margarine-heat in frying pan
1 tablespoon chopped onion cook until transparent
1 tablespoon chopped green pepper
Stir in
2 cups cubed cooked ham
1-(10 ounce) can condensed cream of celery soup
¾ cup milk
1/3 cup mayonnaise
1/3 cup canned, sliced mushrooms
1 teaspoon curry powder

Heat thoroughly but do not boil. Serve over cooked rice or noodles.
Garnish with parsley. Serves 6.

SAUERKRAUT PORK HOCKS AND RICE DINNER

3 to 4 pork hocks 1 pork steak cut into lengthwise about ½ inch thickness
Cook together and then add sauerkraut (approximately 2- 14 ounce can or
756 ml can) Add 1 whole chopped onion

About half way when meat is done add 2 cups long grain rice to meat
and sauerkraut mixture. This dish will last for up to a week in cold, cold
refrigerator.

Very good on hot day in summer.

When someone drops a coin, pick it up and give it to another person. This
will add laughter and bring a smile to one who needs it the most.

TOURTIERE (Meat Pie)

2 pounds ground pork
1 pound lean ground beef
2 cups water
2 cinnamon sticks
1 onion, ground
½ teaspoon salt and garlic salt
¼ teaspoon cayenne pepper. Cloves and allspice
1 bay leaf
¼ teaspoon pepper
2 tablespoons celery leaves
3 large potatoes, cooked and mashed
Pastry for 2 (9 inch) double crust pies

Simmer meat, water and cinnamon sticks together for 45 minutes. Add onion, salts, pepper, cayenne pepper, cloves, allspice, bay leaf and celery leaves. Continue cooking for 15 minutes. Remove bay leaf and cinnamon sticks. Put mixture in pie crusts. Make slits in top of crusts. Bake at 400 Degree oven for 30 minutes.

Pies may be served hot or cold.

PORK CUTLET SUPREME

4or 5 pork cutlets

Cook and simmer cutlets on low in olive oil. When pierced add fresh mushrooms, canned mushroom soup, diced onion, chopped parsley.

When all is cooked add 1 to 2 teaspoons of cornstarch to thicken. Add a bit of water so the meat will not be to filled with water from the fresh mushroom. This mixture is served well with cooked mashed potatoes and vegetable of your choice. Fried zucchini or broccoli adds quite a flavorful aroma when serving this cutlet supreme dinner.

Never change your hairdo, your spouse may not recognize you when he or she comes home.

HAM AND BEAN GREEN CASSEROLE

Sauce:

½ cup margarine   ½ cup flour

3 cups milk   1–½ cup grated cheese

Add a pinch of cayenne pepper to taste

Melt margarine, stir in flour, add milk. Stir over low heat till thickened
Add cheese. Allow to melt.

3 medium potatoes in greased casserole. Cover with green beans. Pour half of
cheese sauce over beans. Cover with ham. Add remaining cheese sauce. Put
bread crumbs on top. Bake at 350 Degree oven for 30 minutes.

Never dig into your deep jean pockets when you are handling a knife. The
knife can cause a big stream of pennies falling onto your toes.

FISH

ALMANDINE FISH FILLETS

4- 8 ounce fillet of cod, snapper or halibut
¼ cup slivered almonds
½ teaspoon garlic powder
½ teaspoon salt
¼ teaspoon pepper
4 – tablespoon lemon juice
5 to 4 tablespoon olive oil
6 lemon wedges

Preheat oven to 350 Degree F. Toast almonds in oven for 5 minutes or until brown Set aside. Meanwhile, season fish on all sides with garlic, salt and pepper.

In skillet, heat oil over medium heat, add fish and cook for 5 minutes. Flip over and Continue cooking until fish is cooked example; when flesh starts to flake when pressure is applied with thumb of fork. Transfer to serving platter. Drizzle with lemon juice and sprinkle with almonds over top.
Serve with lemon wedges.

CRAB FETTUCCINE ALFREDO

½ butter, melted
½ cup heavy cream
1/3 cup shredded mozzarella cheese
1 teaspoon chopped parsley

1 pkg. imitation crab
meat, chunk style
3 cups cooked fettucine noodles
¼ cup parmesan cheese

Combine butter, cream, mozzarella cheese and cook over low heat until cheese melts and cream bubbles and thickens.

Add parsley and crab. Stir and heat until meat is heated through. Arrange Fettuccine noodles on a large plate or shallow dish. Pour mixture over noodles and garnish with parsley and parmesan cheese. Serve at once. Serves 4.

In everyone's walk through life, eating healthy is definitely the wisest thing to do.

Crab or Tuna Salad Pitas

4 ounces of tuna or crab
¼ cup diced cucumber
1 medium sized roma tomato, seeded and diced
¼ teaspoon dill weed
¼ teaspoon celery salt
Yogurt cheese
Small pita bread 3 -inch size. About 7.5 cm size

Yogurt cheese:

28 ounces of non-fat yogurt
Make sure there is no gelatin in yogurt

Line a plastic strainer with a double thickness of cheesecloth. Place over deep bowl. Spoon in yogurt. Cover loosely with plastic wrap. Drain in refrigerator for 24 hours, discarding whey in bowl several times. Remove to sealable container. Cover. Can be stored in fridge until date of expiration.

Break up tuna or crab with fork in medium bowl. Toss with cucumber, tomato, dill weed and celery salt. Stir in yogurt cheese.
Tear open pitas on one side. Fill with ¼ cup tuna or crab mixture. Makes about 6 pitas. Very healthy.

Never go golfing when you start making bread, the yeast might turn into beer or a bear.

CREAMY TUNA CASSEROLE

Preheat oven to 350 Degree F.

Grease a 2 quart casserole. Cook noodles according to package details. 8 -ounces noodles equivalent- ¾ of 12 ounce package.

Combine 2(7 ounce) cans flaked light tuna or fresh tuna
2 (7 -1/2 ounce cans tomato sauce)

Mix together 2 cups cottage cheese
1 (8 ounce) package cream cheese
1/3 cup finely chopped onion
1/3 cup finely chopped raw carrot
½ teaspoon dried parsley flakes
¼ teaspoon basil

Arrange half of the cooked noodles in prepared casserole. Cover with half of cheese mixture, then half of tuna mixture. Repeat layers: for a zesty flavor add ¼ cup of parmesan cheese.

Bake in preheated 350 Degree oven for 45 minutes or until nicely browned. Makes about 8 servings.

Jack and Jill went to a dance and found out they didn't find romance.

SALMON LOAF

1 can salmon or 1 fresh salmon	1 cup cracker crumbs
2- egg yolks, well beaten	1 teaspoon chopped parsley
1 tablespoon lemon juice	2 egg whites, beaten stiff
2- tablespoon butter melted in ½ cup hot milk	

Remove skin and bones from salmon. Add all ingredients except egg whites. Fold in beaten egg whites at the end of all ingredients. Bake in buttered casserole At 350 Degree oven for 1 hour.

TUNA MELT TOAST

4 slices of whole wheat bread
4 - Teaspoons Margarine (Optional)
4 ounce can white tuna or fresh tuna cut up and deveined
5 Fresh asparagus, cooked or 1 can, 12 ounce – 341 ml, drained
1 egg whites large
¼ cup light salad dressing
1 tablespoon chili sauce
Paprika, sprinkle

Toast the bread slices. Spread one side of each with 1 teaspoon margarine If desired. Spread ¼ of tuna on buttered side of each slice of toast. Top with Asparagus. Place on baking sheets.

Beat egg whites in medium bowl until very stiff. Fold in dressing and chili sauce.

Divide and spread egg white mixture right to the edges over tuna and asparagus.

Sprinkle with paprika. Bake in 400 Degree oven on center rack for 8 minutes until meringue topping is golden. Cut into diagonally into 4 pieces.

Never let yourself bark at an old fool, he may be smarter than you.

MARINATED SCALLOPS AND SHRIMPS

8 cups water
1 – ½ clove garlic diced
3 stalks of celery with leaves
¼ teaspoon cayenne

½ cup chopped and diced onion
1 bay leaf
1- ½ tablespoons salt

Bring to boil and simmer for 5 to 7 minutes or until shrimp and scallops are fully cooked. Allow to cool in the broth.

Rub into a large bowl with garlic. Mix together in bowl
¼ cup chopped celery
1 green onion diced or chopped
1 tablespoon chopped chives
6 tablespoons olive oil
1 tablespoons lemon juice
¼ teaspoon Tabasco sauce
1 tablespoons chili sauce
2 tablespoons ketchup
2 tablespoons horse radish
1 tablespoon prepared mustard
1/8 teaspoon paprika

Stir in drained shrimp and scallops and let stand overnight or 24 hours before serving.

When you feel all is lost, remember just try to take a step back and maybe the thought will come back right to you.

EVIE'S DELIGHTFUL STUFFED MUSHROOM CRAB

2 bags of fresh mushroom caps
1 package of Philadelphia Original Cream Cheese
(Optional) 1 package sour cream mixed with ¼ cup milk
(Optional) Adding 3 tablespoons of dry sherry enhances all flavors
1 tablespoon dried onion flakes
¼ teaspoon garlic powder
½ teaspoon dried parsley flakes
Dash of cayenne (Optional: ¼ teaspoon white pepper)

Blend in 1 can of crab or use frozen crab into cavity of mushroom caps.

Bake on greased baking sheets in a preheated oven of 400 Degree F. oven for 6 minutes, or until delicately browned.

Oven-Baked Halibut Steak

4 to 5 halibut
¼ cup soft butter
2 tablespoons finely chopped fresh parsley
2 teaspoons finely chopped dill or dill weed
1 tablespoon dry white wine
Pinch of garlic powder

Add all ingredients to 1 to 2 cups flour. Coat halibut steak evenly around both Sides of fish. Coat and line large pan evenly with soft butter so halibut steak Doesn't stick to pan. Bake until lightly browned pierce steak until you see that it starts to flake.

Serve with any kind of rice and vegetable.

Just remember never to let mighty mouse eat all your fish.

SOUP

CREAM OF BROCCOLI SOUP

6 to 8 teaspoons butter
1 tablespoon chopped onion
1 cup of chicken broth or use chicken broth soup base
¼ teaspoon salt or to taste
Dash of pepper
5 tablespoons flour
2 cups milk

Saute butter and onion. Blend in flour, gradually add broth, milk, salt and pepper, stirring until smooth. Cook until thickened. Puree broccoli in blender. Add to mixture and heat 3 to 4 minutes. Hint: A pinch of curry gives off a flavoring all of its own.

BROCCOLI CHEESE SOUP

1 cup (250 ml) thinly sliced carrot
2 Tablespoons (30 ml) water
10 ounces (300 grams) frozen chopped broccoli
2 ½ cups milk (625 ml)
¼ cup (60 ml) all purpose flour
2 teaspoons (10 ml) chicken bouillon cubes or powder
½ teaspoon (2 ml) salt
¼ teaspoon pepper (1 ml)
1 cup water (250 ml)
1 cup grated medium cheddar cheese

Place carrot and first amount of water in 2 quart (2L) microwave safe casserole cover. Microwave on high (100%) for about 3 minutes until tender.

Add broccoli, cover. Microwave on high (100%) for 2 minutes until tender. Add milk stir.

Combine flour, bouillon powder, salt and peeper in small bowl. Add ½ of second amount of water. Mix until smooth. Add remaining half of water. Pour over carrot mixture. Cover. Microwave on high (100%) for about 6 minutes. Stirring at 1 minute intervals until mixture is boiling and thickened. Add cheese. Stir until cheese is melted. Makes 4 ¾ cups (1.2 L)

Never pick your nose it may start looking like Pinocchio's wooden nose.

BORSCHT

Reserved beet juice
2 - Pockets low sodium beef bouillon powder (1/4 ounce 65 grams each)
3 ½ cups boiling water
2 cups coarsely grated cabbage, lightly packed
1 cup onion
1 cup thinly sliced carrot
1/8 teaspoon ground cloves
1/8 teaspoon dill weed
1/8 teaspoon pepper
14 ounce can diced beets drain and reserve juice

Put reserved beet juice into medium saucepan; bring to a boil. Add bouillon powder and boiling water. Stir to dissolve. Add next six ingredients. Stir. Bring to boil. Cover. Simmer for about, 25 minutes until carrot is tender. Add beets. Return to boiling just until beets are heated.

Stir with dollop of yogurt or use sour cream.

CABBAGE SOUP

1 teaspoon margarine or butter
1 teaspoon vegetable oil
5 cups coarsely shredded cabbage
1 cup carrot slices, ½ inch thick
¾ cup thinly sliced onions
½ celery sliced
1 cup potatoes cubed
4 cups water
2 cups of chicken or turkey broth
1 teaspoon salt
¼ teaspoon dried thyme leaves
¼ teaspoon pepper
¼ teaspoon dried marjoram leaves

In a large quart saucepan- 6-8 size, heat butter and oil over moderately high heat. Add vegetables. Cook 4-5 min., until cabbage begins to wilt. Add remaining ingredients and bring to a boil. Stir, lower heat, cover and simmer for 40 minutes.

Never let a good man leave, until you ask him to go out on a date!

EASY CREAM OF POTATO SOUP

8 slices of bacon cut up   1 cup onion

2 medium potatoes   1 cup water

1 can cream of chicken soup   1 ½ cup milk

Salt and pepper to taste

Chopped parsley

In large stock or quart pan, fry bacon to crisp. Add onion, cook 2-3 minutes. Pour off fat. Add water and potato cubes, simmer until potatoes are tender. Stir in soup, milk, salt, pepper and parsley. Heat to serve. Do not boil.

HANGOVER SOUP

1 ½ pounds hamburger brown then strain and drain fat. Add 4 or more cups water.

1 onion

1 ½ cups cabbage

1 cup celery

1 can tomato or use 4 fresh tomatoes cut and chopped

3 peeled and cut up carrots

2 or 3 medium sized potatoes

1 package Lipton Onion Soup Mix or ½ package use according to your own taste.

HINT: V8 juice goes real well into this soup base. Adds more flavor.

Never say never for tis a wise man will always say or forever stay near you in life.

MUSHROOM SOUP

3 cups sliced fresh mushrooms
1 tablespoon margarine
1 cup water
13 ½ ounce evaporated milk
2 teaspoons Chicken bouillon powder
¼ teaspoon paprika
¼ teaspoon garlic powder
¼ teaspoon salt Sprinkle pepper to taste

Combine mushrooms and margarine in 8 cup 12 litre pan. Cover and cook over low heat and stir until soft.
Add next 9 ingredients. Stir. Process on blender. Return to cook watch your timing for evaporated will sometimes curdle. Cook on low so all flavors are well blended.

FRENCH ONION SOUP

6 Tablespoons margarine
2 ½ pounds onions sliced about 7
1 tablespoon granulated sugar
2 tablespoons All purpose flour
1/8 teaspoon salt ¼ teaspoon pepper
7 - 1/5 ounce beef bouillon cubes
8 cups boing water
8 slices of French Bread, toasted and cubed
2 cups grated Gruyere cheese

Melt margarine in frying pan. Add onion and brown sugar. Saute slowly until medium brown in color, stirring often. Sprinkle with flour, salt and pepper. Stir and cook for 5 minutes. Dissolve beef bouillon cubes in boiling water in large saucepan. Add contents of frying pan. Bring to a boil. Simmer covered for 20 minutes.

Anything is possible in life, just making a small change will brighten your livelihood.

BAKED GOODS-COOKIES, CAKES, PIES AND PUDDINGS

CHEWY OATMEAL RAISIN COOKIES

1 cup packed light brown sugar
1 cup margarine softened
1 egg
1 teaspoon vanilla extract
2 cups quick cooking oats
1 ½ cups all purpose flour
1 teaspoon baking soda
1 teaspoon pumpkin pie spice
1 cup seedless raisins

In large bowl with electric mixer or medium speed, beat sugar and margarine until blended. Beat in egg and vanilla until mixture is smooth. Blend in oats, flour, baking soda and pumpkin pie spice. Stir in raisins.

Drop batter by table spoonfuls, 2 inches apart, onto greased baking sheets. Bake at 400 Degree F. for 5 to 7 minutes or until lightly browned. Remove from sheets; cool on wire racks. Makes about 3 dozen.

GRANDMA EVIE'S GINGERSNAPS

1 ½ cup shortening or margarine
2 cups sugar
2 eggs
1/3 cup cooking molasses
4 cups flour
3 teaspoons baking soda
2 tablespoons cinnamon
1 teaspoon salt

Preheat oven to 350 Degree F. Cream shortening. Add sugar. Beat in eggs. Add sifted dry ingredients. Mix well. Form into balls, roll in sugar.

Bake on ungreased cookie sheet for 10 to 12 minutes. Do not over bake.

When you go shopping, don't get to close to the butcher. He might make eye contact and wink at you.

HOME MADE GRAHAM WAFERS

4 cups whole wheat flour   1 egg, slightly beaten
1 cup butter   ½ cup hot water (approximately)
1 cup brown sugar   Unbleached white flour
1 teaspoon baking soda
1 teaspoon cream of tartar

Preheat oven to 350F. Put whole wheat flour, sugar, baking soda and cream of tartar in bowl. Cut in butter until mixture is consistency of coarse oatmeal. Add egg and enough hot water to make a dough that can be rolled like pastry.

Roll out dough to 1/8 to ¼ inch thick on floured pastry board or cloth. (Use unbleached white flour for rolling.) Cut into 3 inch squares, place on ungreased baking sheet and bake 15 to 20 minutes or until done. Cool.

Makes about 2 dozen cookies.

TRADITIONAL SUGAR COOKIES

¾ cup shortening (part bitter softened)
1 cup sugar
2 eggs
1 teaspoon vanilla
2 ½ cups flour
1 teaspoon baking powder
1 teaspoon salt

Mix thoroughly shortening, sugar, eggs and vanilla. Blend in flour, baking powder and salt. Cover, chill at least 1 hour. Heat oven to 400 Degree F.

Roll dough 1/8 inch thick on lightly floured board. Cut into desired sheet. Bake 6 to 8 minutes or until lightly browned. Makes about 4 dozen, 3 inch cookies.

Never tell a man or woman they stink, they might throw a stink bomb at you.

NO BAKE ALLIGATOR COOKIES

½ cup butter
½ cup milk
2 cups sugar
Pinch of salt
4 Tablespoons cocoa
3 cups rolled oats
½ cup peanut butter
1 teaspoon vanilla

Boil first 5 ingredients well for 1 minute. Remove from heat; add rolled oats, peanut butter and vanilla. Drop by spoon- ful's onto cookie sheet that is covered with wax paper. After they have cooled, you may find that are shaped like alligators.

OLD FASHIONED OATMEAL COOKIES

1 cup margarine	1 teaspoon baking soda
1 cup brown sugar	1 teaspoon baking powder
1 cup white sugar	3 cups oatmeal
2 eggs	1 ½ cup flour
1 teaspoon salt	¾ cup coconut
1 teaspoon vanilla	¾ finely chopped walnuts or pecans

Preheat oven to 350 Degree F. Cream margarine, sugar and eggs. Add other ingredients and mix well. Roll into small balls and flatten with fork. Bake for 12 to 15 minutes or until nicely browned.

Better watch where you walk along a dirt road, a toad might jump right into your path and land on to your arm.

PEANUT BUTTER COOKIES

1 egg
½ cup butter
½ cup white sugar
½ cup brown sugar
1 cup flour
½ teaspoon soda or baking powder

Cream butter and sugar, add egg and beat well. Add peanut butter and mix. Sift soda and flour and add to mixture. Roll in small balls, put in cookie sheet, press down with fork. Bake in medium oven 300 to 350 Degree oven.

SOUR CREAM COOKIES

1 cup sugar
1 cup butter
1 teaspoon soda
1 egg
3 cups flour
1 teaspoon nutmeg
Sour cream

Blend dry ingredients with butter till crumbs. Beat egg and cream and add. Roll and then cut out and bake in oven at 350 Degree till cooked.

Better watch out for someone may be watching and looking at you through the looking glass.

WHEAT GERM COOKIES

½ cup oil
1 cup sugar
1 egg
1 teaspoon baking powder
1 cup wheat germ
1 cup flour
½ teaspoon soda
1 teaspoon vanilla

Mix together and roll in small balls. Place 2 inches apart on greased cookie sheet. Press with fork. Watch for they bake quickly. Bake at 350 Degree for 6 minutes.

WHIPPED SHORT BREAD COOKIES

2 cups butter (450ml)
1 cup Icing Sugar (225 ml)
1 cup Cornstarch
3 cups flour

Combine all at high speed in electric mixer at high speed. These whipped shortbread cookies are baked in low oven at 325 Degree. Watch so they won't burn.

Cool on wire rack.

Always keep a positive attitude, for no one likes a negative male or female.

MUFFINS AND CAKES

APPLE BRAN MUFFINS

TOPPINGS
½ cup lightly packed brown sugar
1/3 cup flour
2 tablespoons butter or margarine

The first three ingredients are made separate and combined together to make a crumble like texture. This is the topping to which is added to each individual muffin before baking in the oven.

Sift together 1 ¼ cup flour
½ cup whole bran flakes
¼ cup granulated sugar
3 teaspoons baking powder
1/3 teaspoon salt
½ teaspoon cinnamon
Beat together
1 egg
¼ cup milk
3 tablespoons vegetable oil or melted shortening

Add liquid to dry ingredients and stir only until combined. (Batter will be lumpy) Fill prepared muffin cups 2/3 full. Top each muffin with 1 teaspoon applesauce.

Sprinkle with reserved crumbs. Bake in 400 Degree oven for 18 to 20 minutes or until golden brown. Makes 12 muffins.

Never judge an old book by its color, it may be the best thing you can read.

BLUEBERRY MUFFINS

1 egg
½ cup sugar
½ cup milk
¼ cup vegetable oil
2 teaspoons baking powder
1 ½ cups flour
½ teaspoon salt
1 cup fresh blueberries, drained

Heat oven to 400 Degree F. Grease bottom of baking cups or use paper baking cups.

Beat egg with fork. Stir in milk and oil. Blend in combined dry ingredients, stirring just until flour is moistened. Batter will be lumpy. Do not over-mix. Fold in blueberries. Fill muffin cups 2/3 full. Bake 20-25 minutes or until golden brown. Loosen immediately with spatula. Yield 12 muffins.

MORNING GLORY MUFFINS

2 ½ cups sugar 4 cups shredded carrots
2 apples shredded 1 cup pecans
6 eggs, lightly beaten 2 cups vegetable oil
1 teaspoon vanilla 1 cup shredded coconut
4 cups flour
4 teaspoons cinnamon
4 teaspoons baking soda

Sift together into a bowl, the sugar, flour, cinnamon, baking soda. Add coconut, carrots, apples and pecans. Stir well add eggs, oil and vanilla. Stir until blended.

Spoon into greased muffin tins and bake in a large pre-heated 375 Degree F. Oven for 20 minutes.

Too much wining and dining will or might wreck havoc with your love life.

BANANA MUFFINS

1 ¾ cups flour
1 teaspoon baking soda
¼ teaspoon salt
½ cup melted butter
1 cup white sugar
1 teaspoon cinnamon
2 eggs
¼ cup sour cream
3 mashed bananas

Beat eggs, sugar and butter together. In a separate bowl, combine flour, soda and salt. Stir into first mixture. Finally mix in the sour cream and mashed bananas. Line a 12 muffin tin with large size baking cups and divide mixture evenly. Bake in a preheated 400 Degree F. oven for approximately 2 minutes, A toothpick inserted into a muffin should come out cleanly when muffins are finished cooking.

HEALTHY HEARTY MUFFINS

1 egg
¼ cup applesauce
½ cup skim milk
1/3 cup molasses
2 mashed bananas
1/2 cup whole wheat flour
1 ½ cups oat bran
½ cup raisins
½ cup chopped apricots
½ cup walnuts crushed
1 teaspoon baking powder
1 teaspoon baking soda

Mix all ingredients together and bake in paper lined muffin tins at 375 Degree F. for 15 to 20 minutes.

Never tell dirty jokes while your trying to do a clean up job in the kitchen.

BANANA CAKE

½ cup shortening
1 ¼ cups white sugar
2 eggs
1 teaspoon vanilla extract
2 ¼ cups flour
2 teaspoons baking powder
1 teaspoon baking soda
½ teaspoon salt
1 cup ripe mashed banana
¾ cup buttermilk

Preheat oven to 350 Degree F. Grease two 8 inch round pans. Cream shortening and beat in sugar. Blend in eggs and vanilla and beat until light and fluffy. Set aside. Sift together dry ingredients and add to creamed mixture alternately with bananas and buttermilk. Make three dry and two liquid additions. Combine lightly after each addition. Turn into greased pans and bake for 30 to 35 minutes. Cool 5 minutes and remove from pan. Let cool completely and frost with Banana Icing.

BANANA ICING

½ cup butter
½ cup mashed ripe banana
3 ½ cups icing sugar
1 tablespoon lemon juice
1 teaspoon vanilla extract

Cream together the butter and the banana, gradually blend in the remaining ingredients. Chill until spreading of consistency.

Remember never tell tall tales of rubber, it might come and bounce right back to you.

CARROT CAKE

1 small can crushed pineapple
3 eggs
2 cups sugar
1 ½ cups cooking oil
2 cups grated carrots
3 cups flour
1 teaspoon baking soda
½ teaspoon salt
1 teaspoon baking powder
1 teaspoon nutmeg and cinnamon
2 teaspoons vanilla

Cream egg, oil, sugar add carrots, vanilla and pineapple. Dry ingredients are sifted at least 3 or 4 times and beat in slowly to first mixture. 1 cup nuts are added last.

Bake 75 minutes at 350 Degree F. oven.

CHOCOLATE CAKE

2 cups flour
1 ¾ cups sugar
¼ cup cocoa
1 tablespoon baking soda
1 egg
2/3 cup oil
1 cup sour milk (mix 1 teaspoon lemon juice or vinegar into milk)
1 cup cold strong coffee

Cake: Mix dry ingredients, add liquids. Bake 40 minutes at 350 Degree F. in 9x12 pan.

Icing: Mix 2 ½ tablespoons flour and ½ cup milk. Cook over medium heat until it forms a paste. Let cool. When cake is ready to ice, add to paste: ½ cup sugar,1/2 teaspoon vanilla, ½ cup margarine, 2 tablespoons cocoa. Mix well.

A wise man once said: Better not run faster than your buns can take you!

CHOCOLATE DELIGHT

1 cup flour ½ cup chopped nuts
½ cup butter

Mix and press into cake pan. Bake at 350 Degrees for 15 minutes. Cool.
8 -ounce package cream cheese ½ cup powdered sugar
1/3 cup peanut butter ¾ cup whipped topping

Whip topping and pour into the rest of the ingredients. Pour mixture on top of baked crust.

1 package vanilla instant pudding
1 package chocolate instant pudding
4 cups milk

Beat together and pour on top of cream cheese mixture. Beat 1 ½ cups whipped topping and spread on top. Sprinkle with nuts and chocolate chips.

The best things in life can be free, just remember to drink your tea.

LEMON POPPY SEED CHIFFON

½ cup poppy seeds
1 cup water

In a bowl sift:

2 cups sifted flour
3 tablespoons baking powder
1 ½ cups sugar
½ teaspoon salt

Form a well and add to dry ingredients:
½ cup vegetable oil
1 teaspoon vanilla
1 ½ teaspoon lemon extract
Poppy seeds with water
10 unbeaten egg yolks
½ baking soda

Beat until smooth.

In another deep bowl put:

10 egg whites
¼ teaspoon cream of tartar

Beat egg whites until stiff peaks form. Gently pour yolk mixture into whites and fold in.

Do not stir. Pour into ungreased tube pan. Bake for 50 minutes at 325 Degree F. then increase temperature to 350 Degree F. Bake for 15 minutes longer. Turn pan upside down to cool.

When whipping anything in a blender don't put your nose to close. It may be beaten!

97

NEVER FAIL CHEESECAKE

1 – 8 ounce package cream cheese
1 cup icing sugar
1 teaspoon vanilla
1 cup whipping cream, whipped

Mix first three ingredients well, in blender. Blend in whipped cream. Place in baked cooled graham wafer crust. Place any kind of berry of your choice. My favorite is blueberry: frozen or fresh put into pan and cook with 1 teaspoon of sherry. This sherry gives an exotic flavor to any type of berry.

Always remember to never flirt with a brown-noser.

PIES

APPLE-RHUBARB PIE

1 to 1 ½ cups granulated sugar
1/3 cup flour

Mix together
2 ½ cups rhubarb (1 inch pieces)   2 cups apples, diced
1 teaspoon cinnamon Pinch of salt
½ tablespoon butter

Make pie dough and glaze top with egg white add a bit of cinnamon sugar sparingly.

Make slits for pie to vent. Bake in oven at 350 degree for 40 to 45 minutes.

EVIE'S IMPOSSIBLE PIE

4 eggs   ½ cup margarine
1 cup sugar   2 teaspoons vanilla
1 teaspoon almond extract   ½ cup flour
2 cups milk   1 ½ cups coconut
Pinch of nutmeg

Mix all ingredients in blender. Pour mixture into greased 10 inch deep pie pan. Bake at 350 Degree oven for 1 hour or until center tests firm. The flour will make the crust, coconut forms the topping and center is a custard filling.

Don't flap your mouth at a stranger, he might flap back.

FLAPPER PIE

Crumb Crust
1 ¼ cups graham wafer crumbs
¼ cup sugar
1/3 cup melted butter
Bake 1 ½ minutes on HIGH in microwave or 8 minutes in 375 Degree F. oven.

Filling:
½ cup granulated sugar
2 tablespoons cornstarch
1 tablespoon flour
¼ teaspoon salt
2 cups milk
2 egg, yolks, slightly beaten
1 tablespoon butter
1 teaspoon vanilla

In saucepan combine sugar, cornstarch, flour and salt. Stir in milk. Cook over moderate heat, stirring constantly until mixture thickens and comes to a boil. Add egg yolks. Cook 1 minute longer. Blend in butter and vanilla. Cool to room temperature before putting on meringue.

When you feel all is lost, then you might be able to find it when you take a longer lasting thought with contemplation.

NEVER FAIL MERINGUE

1 tablespoon cornstarch   2 tablespoons cold water
½ cup boiling water   3 egg whites
6 tablespoons sugar   1 teaspoon vanilla
Pinch of salt

Blend cornstarch and cold water in a saucepan. Add boiling water and cook, stirring until clear and thickened. Let stand until completely cold. With electric beater at high speed, beat egg whites until foamy. Gradually add sugar and beat until stiff but not dry. Turn mixer to low speed, add salt and vanilla. Gradually beat in cornstarch mixture. Turn mixer again to high speed and beat well. Spread meringue. Bake at 350 Degree for about 10 minutes. This meringue cuts beautifully and never gets sticky.

FRESH BERRY PIE

Mix together:
¾ cup granulated sugar
¼ cup flour
Pinch of salt (Hint: adding a ½ teaspoon of vanilla brings more flavor to pie)

Combine with:
4 ¼ cup berries
Turn into pastry filled pie plate. Dot with: 1 tablespoon butter or margarine.

Cover with top pie crust. Seal and flute edges. Make sure you make slits in top pie crust.

Preheat oven to 450 degree. Add pie to oven cook for 15 minutes and then turn down oven to 350 degree. Bake for 50 to 55 minutes.

Remember to never tell no lies, it may become bigger than the widest ocean.

MY DUTCH APPLE PIE

5 cups peeled sliced apples
Soak in apple juice so they won't turn brown
Combine:
¼ cup granulated sugar
¼ cup brown sugar
3 tablespoons flour
Stir in and beat with rotary beater until smooth add 1 cup thick sour cream.
Pour sour cream to apples and brown sugar.

Put all into a 9 inch pie plate which has been lined with pie dough.

Put pie into preheated 400 Degree oven for 15 minutes, turn oven down to 350 and bake for another 35 to 40 minutes. Oh so yummy when you add a little bit of cinnamon sugar to top of pie before you put in oven.

Never pick berries by yourself, some of those wild stinging bees might jump full force at you.

PEACH PIE COBBLER

4 cups sliced peaches
Combine:
¾ cup granulated sugar
3 tablespoons flour
½ teaspoon cinnamon
Pinch of nutmeg

Preheat oven to 450 Degree. Prepare pastry dough for pie. Line a 9 inch pie plate, trim.

Blanch peaches in boiling water for 1 minute, place in cold water. Remove skins and stones. Slice sufficient to make 4 cups sliced peaches. Instead of using pie dough for top. Try using a ½ cup margarine, ½ cup brown sugar with ½ teaspoon of cinnamon, 2/3 cups oatmeal and ½ cup flour. Blend all together and make a mixture of coarse crumbly and put on top of peaches.

Put in preheated oven for 15 minutes till golden and then turn oven down to 350 and bake for 30 to 35 minutes.

When off in the distance, a brown cow mooed at your funny singing voice.

PUMPKIN PIE

2/3 cup brown sugar   1 teaspoon cinnamon

1 teaspoon ginger   ½ teaspoon salt

¼ cup water   1 ¼ cup pumpkin

2 eggs, beaten   1 cup cream

1/3 cup orange juice

Blend sugar, spices and water. Stir in eggs and pumpkin. Add cream and juice. Pour into unbaked pie shell. Bake at 450 Degree F. oven for 1 Minutes, then turn down oven to 350 Degree F for 40 to 50 minutes.

Makes 1 large pie.

APPLE RICE PUDDING

4 large peeled and cored apples
1 cup large grain rice
¼ cup sugar
1 teaspoon vanilla
1 teaspoon cinnamon
Optional: ½ cup raisins
2 cups water 2 cups apple-juice

Combine all in saucepan, cook on low heat till all is done. This serves well with ice cream or any type of whipping cream.

GLAZED BANANAS

Peel bananas whole saturate banana with honey.
Then sprinkle slivered almonds on top of honeyed banana.
Bake in oven till almonds are lightly browned

Do this on low oven, 300-325 Degree
ENJOY

Make sure you don't eat too many bananas, you might just go ape.

BREADS

BANNOCK

3 cups flour
3 ½ teaspoons baking powder
Pinch of salt
¼ cup oil (NOTE: warm water is added to oil to make 1 cup of liquid)

Preheat oven to 375 Degree F. Mix your oil and lukewarm water to make 1 cup of liquid.

Pour over all the other ingredients in a bowl and knead. Your dough should be light and not dry or sticky. Flatten with hands in a 12- inch pie plate. Poke with a fork to make air holes.

Bake until golden brown.

BUNS

Soak 1 tablespoon yeast with 1 teaspoon sugar and ½ cup warm water for 10 minutes.
5 or 6 beaten eggs
½ cup sugar
1 cup Mazola oil (or which ever oil you prefer)
3 or more cups of scalded milk with some water.
1 tablespoon salt
3 tablespoons vinegar
Add the yeast, 10 or more cups of flour to make a soft dough.

Let stand at room temperature to rise for 2 hours. Knead down slightly and shape into buns, Let rise an hour more. Bake 15 minutes in a 400 Degree oven. Yield about 6 dozen.

This bun recipe is one of my favorites.

Tis the season for some common reason.

EVIE'S EASY LOAF BREAD

2 ¾ cup milk
¼ cup granulated sugar
2 teaspoons salt
1/3 cup shortening (hint: what I find healthier to use is butter or margarine then the salt is already added in, so no need for extra salt)
Add all together and melt, cool to lukewarm. When lukewarm add 1 beaten egg.

Meanwhile, dissolve 1 tablespoon sugar in 1 ½ cups lukewarm water(100f) Over this sprinkle 3 envelopes active dry yeast.

Let stand for 10 minutes. Then stir briskly with a fork. Add softened yeast to lukewarm milk mixture. Stir.

Beat in 5 cups flour Beat vigorously by hand or with electric mixer.

Then gradually beat in with a spoon an additional 5 ½ to 6 cups flour Work in last half of flour with a rotating motion of the hand. Turn dough onto a lightly floured surface and knead 8 to 10 minutes. Shape into a smooth ball, cover with wax paper and a dampened cloth with hot water and let rest for 20 minutes. Divide dough into four.

Roll out each portion, pressing out any large bubbles. Fold over and roll up tightly, shaping into loaves. Place in greased 8 ½ x 4 ½ inch loaf pans. Cover with oiled wax paper and a damp cloth and let rise in a warm place until doubled (about 1 ¼ hours) or place in refrigerator for 2 to 24 hours. Remember you have to let refrigerated loaves stand for 20 minutes at room temperature before baking.

An old fisherman lost his shoe, but couldn't find it so he used a canoe.

RAISIN BREAD

Scald 2 cups milk
Mix together ¼ cup granulated sugar
1 teaspoon salt
1 teaspoon cinnamon
Pour hot milk into a large bowl with sugar mixture and add ¼ cup shortening
or margarine. Cool to lukewarm.
Mix in 1 ½ cups raisins

Meanwhile, dissolve 1 teaspoon sugar in ½ cup lukewarm water(100F)
Over this sprinkle 1 envelope active dry yeast. Let stand for 10 minutes. Then
stir briskly with a fork. Add softened yeast to lukewarm milk mixture. Stir
Beat in 2 ½ cups flour. Beat vigorously by hand or use rotary blender. Then
gradually beat in with a wooden spoon an additional 2 ½ to 3 cups flour. Turn
dough onto a lightly floured surface and knead 8 to 10 minutes. Shape into a
smooth ball, cover with wax paper and a dampened cloth with hot water and
let rest for 20 minutes. Divide dough into four.

Roll out each portion, pressing out any large bubbles. Fold over and roll
up tightly, shaping into loaves. Place in greased 8 ½ x 4 ½ inch loaf pans.
Cover with oiled wax paper and a damp cloth and let rise in a warm place
until doubled (about 1 ¼ hours) or place in refrigerator for 2 to 24 hours.
Remember you have to let refrigerated loaves stand for 20 minutes at room
temperature before baking.

Always go to bed with a smile on your face, then you will have sweet dreams.

RYE BREAD

Scald 2 2/3 cups milk or use half water and half milk
Pour into large bowl and then add
½ cup lightly packed brown sugar
2 teaspoons salt
¼ cup shortening or use oil if you prefer
Stir until shortening melts. Cool to lukewarm.

Meanwhile dissolve
2 teaspoons sugar in 1 cup lukewarm water (100F)
Over this sprinkle 2 envelopes of active dry yeast
Let stand for 10 minutes. Then stir briskly with fork. Add softened yeast to lukewarm
Milk mixture. Stir beat in
4 ½ cups dark rye flour
Beat vigorously by hand or use with electric mixer. Then gradually add more white unbleached flour till it becomes firm enough to knead and cover as with the same results as white and raisin bread. Use same temperature as from the other two breads stated above.

ZUCCHINI BREAD

3 eggs
1 cup honey
3 cups flour
2 teaspoons vanilla
1 cup vegetable oil
2 cups shredded zucchini
½ cup nuts or raisins
1 teaspoon soda
1 teaspoon baking powder
1 teaspoon salt
1 ½ teaspoon cinnamon
½ teaspoon nutmeg

Beat eggs, gradually add honey, oil and vanilla. Stir in zucchini; add dry ingredients, nuts and raisins. Bake 350 Degree oven for 45 to 55 minutes.

Parting can be the best thing in life, just remember to leave in a hurry.

Printed in the United States
By Bookmasters